Our Solar System
THE MOON

Mary-Jane Wilkins
Consultant: Giles Sparrow, FRAS

WAYLAND
www.waylandbooks.co.uk

This edition first published in Great Britain in 2017 by Wayland

© 2017 Brown Bear Books Ltd

Wayland
An imprint of Hachette Children's Group
Part of Hodder & Stoughton
Carmelite House
50 Victoria Embankment
London EC4Y 0DZ
An Hachette UK Company
www.hachette.co.uk
www.hachettechildrens.co.uk

ISBN 978 1 5263 0291 5

Brown Bear Books Ltd
First Floor, 9–17 St. Albans Place
London N1 0NX

Author: Mary-Jane Wilkins
Consultant: Giles Sparrow, Fellow of the Royal Astronomical Society
Picture Researcher: Clare Newman
Illustrations: Supriya Sahai
Designer: Melissa Roskell
Design Manager: Keith Davis
Editorial Director: Lindsey Lowe
Children's Publisher: Anne O'Daly

Printed in Malaysia

Websites
The website addresses (URLs) included in this book were valid at the time of going to press. However, it is possible that contents or addresses may change following the publication of this book. No responsibility for any such changes can be accepted by either the author or the Publisher.

Contents

What is the Moon?

A moon is a ball of rock that goes around, or orbits, a planet. Our Moon orbits Earth. It is a cold, dry place where there is no air to breathe.

Sunlight reflected off the Moon reaches Earth in one second.

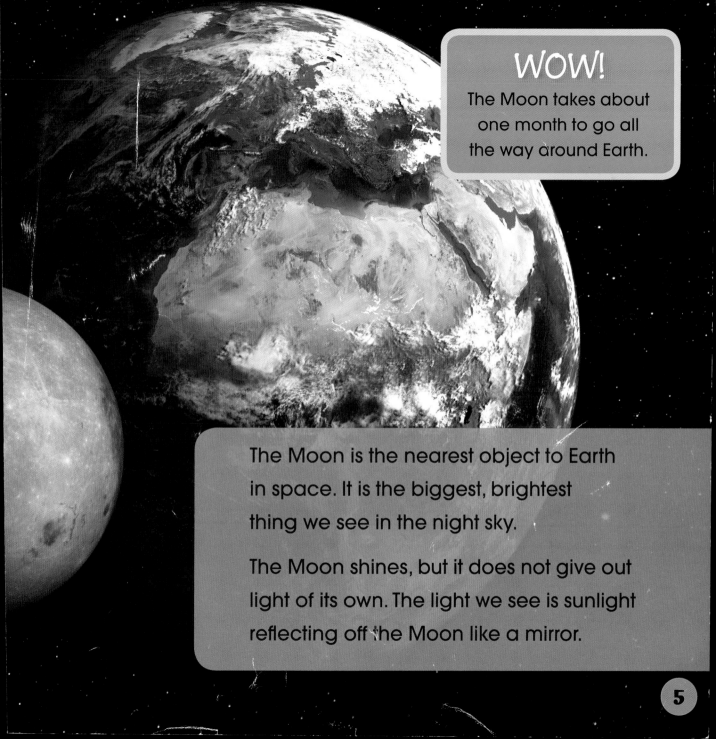

WOW!
The Moon takes about one month to go all the way around Earth.

The Moon is the nearest object to Earth in space. It is the biggest, brightest thing we see in the night sky.

The Moon shines, but it does not give out light of its own. The light we see is sunlight reflecting off the Moon like a mirror.

The solar system

Earth's Moon travels around Earth.
Our planet, Earth, orbits the Sun.
The Sun is the huge shining star
at the centre of our solar system. It gives
out the heat and light we call sunshine.

Mars

Jupiter

Lots of rocks
called asteroids
fly around
the Sun, too.

Mercury

Venus

Earth

Earth's Moon

Seven other planets orbit the Sun.
They are Mercury, Venus, Mars, Jupiter,
Saturn, Uranus and Neptune. Dwarf planets
also orbit the Sun. Pluto is a dwarf planet.
The Sun, the planets and other space
objects make up the solar system.

Uranus

Neptune

Pluto (dwarf planet)

Saturn

How did the Moon form?

Millions of years ago, a planet crashed into Earth. Rock thrown into space by the crash formed the Moon. Some planets have lots of moons. Earth has just one.

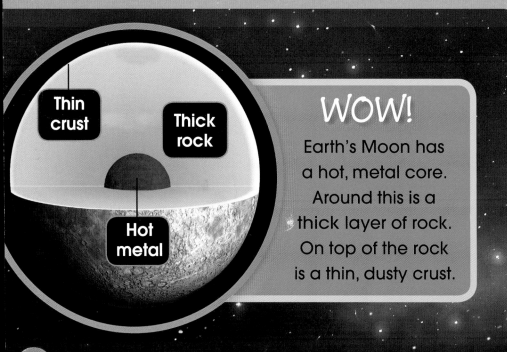

Thin crust

Thick rock

Hot metal

WOW!

Earth's Moon has a hot, metal core. Around this is a thick layer of rock. On top of the rock is a thin, dusty crust.

When the Moon first formed,
it was closer to Earth than it is now.
Every year it moves 3.8 cm further
away from us.

The surface of the Moon

The surface of the Moon has thousands of holes shaped like saucers. They are called craters. They were made by big space rocks crashing into the Moon.

This picture of the Moon was coloured on a computer to show how high the land is. The highest parts are red.

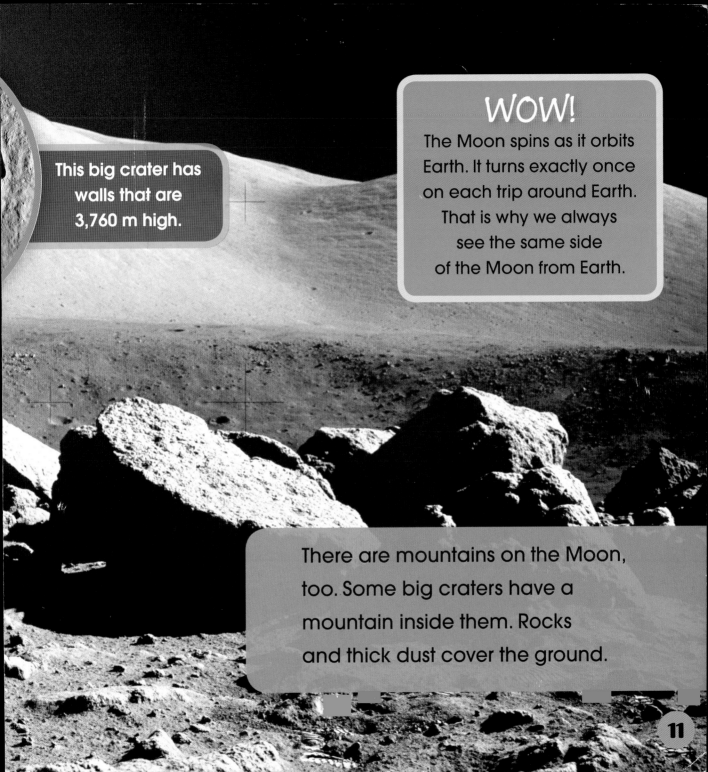

This big crater has walls that are 3,760 m high.

WOW!

The Moon spins as it orbits Earth. It turns exactly once on each trip around Earth. That is why we always see the same side of the Moon from Earth.

There are mountains on the Moon, too. Some big craters have a mountain inside them. Rocks and thick dust cover the ground.

How the Moon changes

The Sun lights up half of the Moon.
We can't see the rest because it is in
shadow. The Moon has different phases.
When we see all of it, we call this a full moon.

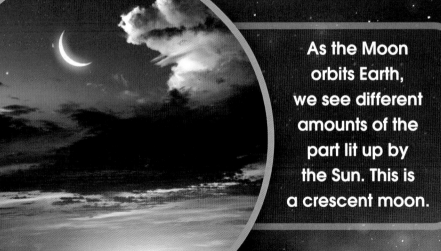

As the Moon orbits Earth, we see different amounts of the part lit up by the Sun. This is a crescent moon.

Full Moon

When the Moon grows bigger from night to night, we say it is waxing. When the Moon grows smaller, we say it is waning.

13

Looking at the Moon

People on Earth have looked at the night sky for thousands of years. A scientist invented the telescope about 400 years ago. It made things look bigger and nearer. This helped people see the night sky more clearly.

The Hubble Space Telescope takes pictures in space.

People who study space and the stars are called astronomers. They look at the sky through big telescopes. Some telescopes are on mountains. They see the sky clearly.

In 1990 scientists sent the huge Hubble Space Telescope into space. It takes photos and sends them back to Earth.

Exploring the Moon

Scientists send probes into space to look at the Moon close up. The probes take photos of the Moon. Some probes have landed on the surface.

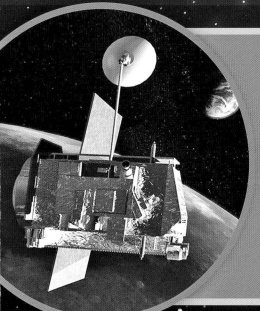

WOW!

Today a spacecraft flies around the Moon taking photos. It is called the *Lunar Reconnaissance Orbiter*. The photos will help scientists make a map of the Moon.

In 1998 a tiny space probe went to look for ice in craters on the Moon. It was only 140 cm wide! The probe crashed at the end of its journey.

Lunar Prospector

People on the Moon

The Moon is the only part of the solar system that people have visited. The first person to land on the Moon was Neil Armstrong in 1969. He travelled there on a spacecraft called *Apollo 11*. Another explorer in *Apollo 11* called Buzz Aldrin walked on the Moon, too.

The men left their footprints on the Moon. The footprints will stay there for millions of years. This is because there is no wind or rain on the Moon.

A space explorer is called an astronaut.

Twelve astronauts have visited the Moon.

They brought Moon rocks back to Earth.

Eclipses

The Moon travels around the Earth.
The Earth orbits the Sun. Sometimes
the Moon, the Earth and the Sun all
line up in a row.

The Moon can
turn red or
orange during
an eclipse.

When the Earth is between the Sun and
the Moon, it makes a shadow on the Moon.
This is called a lunar eclipse. The photo
shows how the Moon disappears when
the shadow of the Earth falls on it.

Make moon phases

What you need

4 chocolate cream-filled
   biscuits (or round crackers
   and cream cheese)

Lolly stick or plastic knife
Sheet of paper

What to do

1. Twist the top of each biscuit. Try not to pull off the cream.

2. Use the lolly stick or plastic knife to scrape off the cream filling. Make your biscuits match the pictures here. They show the shapes of four of the phases of the Moon.

3. Arrange the biscuits on the sheet of paper in order. Write the name of the phase under each biscuit.

First Quarter
(Half Moon)

Full Moon

New Moon

Third Quarter
(Half Moon)

Useful words

asteroid
A big rock that orbits the Sun. An asteroid can be just a few metres across, or hundreds of kilometres wide.

comet
A ball of rock, dust and ice that orbits the Sun.

core
The centre of a star, planet or moon.

crater
A hole in the surface of the Moon made by a large rocky object hitting it.

eclipse
There is an eclipse when one object in space passes in front of another and hides it. In a lunar eclipse, the Earth blocks the Sun's light.

lunar
To do with the Moon.

orbit
To move around another object.

planet
A large object in space that orbits the Sun or another star.

Find out more

Websites
www.planetsforkids.org/moon.html

www.esa.int/esaKIDSen/Planetsandmoons.html

www.spacekids.co.uk/themoon

Books
Fact Cat Moon, Alice Harman (Wayland, 2015)

First Encyclopedia of Space, Paul Dowswell (Usborne, 2010)

First Fabulous Facts Space, Anita Ganeri (Ladybird, 2014)

Index